{ TRIUMPH ON ICE }

JEAN RILEY SENFT

photography by GÉRARD CHÂTAIGNEAU

Triumph on Ice

The New World of Figure Skating

GREYSTONE BOOKS

D&M PUBLISHERS INC.

Vancouver/Toronto/Berkeley

Greystone Books
An imprint of D&M Publishers Inc.
2323 Quebec Street, Suite 201
Vancouver BC Canada V5T 4S7
www.greystonebooks.com

Cataloguing data available from Library and Archives Canada
ISBN 978-1-55365-657-9 (cloth)

Editing by Michelle Benjamin
Copyediting by Pam Robertson
Jacket and text design by Jessica Sullivan
Jacket and interior photographs by Gérard Châtaigneau
Printed and bound in Canada by Friesens
Text printed on acid-free paper
Distributed in the U.S. by Publishers Group West

We gratefully acknowledge the financial support of the Canada Council
for the Arts, the British Columbia Arts Council, the Province of British
Columbia through the Book Publishing Tax Credit, and the Government
of Canada through the Canada Book Fund for our publishing activities.

Mixed Sources
Cert no. SW-COC-001271
© 1996 FSC
FSC

{ CONTENTS }

1   INTRODUCTION: A New Era

5   The Evolution of Figure Skating

13   The ISU Judging System

39   Triumph on Ice

131   CONCLUSION: Where Will Figure Skating Go From Here?

133   Index of Skaters and Coaches

135   Acknowledgments

. . . . .

INTRODUCTION:
A NEW ERA

. . . . .

T HE 2010 Olympic Winter Games in Vancouver, British
Columbia, was an emotionally charged event that showcased
an array of athletic talent. Figure skating was one of the most
dramatic and popular events at the Games, and the Pacific Coliseum, where
skating was held, buzzed with excitement. The competitions were close, and
skaters in all disciplines displayed unprecedented depth, pushing the limits of
athleticism and artistic performance.

Both the Ice Dance and Pair events at the 2010 Games were historic. In Ice
Dance, a stellar performance by Canadians Tessa Virtue and Scott Moir marked
the first time since the event made its Olympic debut in 1976 in Innsbruck that a
Canadian or North American team captured gold. With the exceptions of Jayne
Torvill and Christopher Dean from Great Britain, who won in 1984, and Marina
Anissina and Gwendal Peizerat from France, who won in 2002, ice dancers from
the Soviet Union and Russia have dominated the discipline.

Virtue and Moir's friends and training mates Meryl Davis and Charlie
White from the United States won silver—a thrilling triumph for all four skaters,
and certainly for their shared coaches, Marina Zoueva and Igor Shpilband, both

originally from Russia. The spellbinding performances of Virtue and Moir and of Davis and White were as good as any seen in the history of Ice Dance. Both teams have taken the sport to a new level of speed, risk, intricacy, accuracy of footwork, creativity, and unison.

The Olympic Pair event also indicated that historic changes were happening in the sport. A Pair team from Russia or the Soviet Union had won gold at every Olympics since 1964. In 2010, China's Xue Shen and Hongbo Zhao came out of retirement to try for the gold that had eluded them at the two previous Winter Olympics. Aliona Savchenko and Robin Szolkowy, skating for Germany and the world champions in 2008 and 2009, also aimed to own the podium. When it was all over, three Chinese teams had placed in the top five, giving an indication of Pair power in the future. No Russian team reached the podium in Pairs, and a decades-old dynasty came to an end.

In the Single events, the Korean media reported that the entire nation stopped to watch Yu-Na Kim's Olympic performances. She shone under the tremendous pressure and delivered two flawless skates, strong in all elements and components, and earned record points. She won the gold medal more than 23 points ahead of her nearest competitor—a stellar achievement. Joannie Rochette from Canada touched hearts worldwide when she found the strength to compete two days after the unexpected death of her mother. Evgeni Plushenko of Russia and Evan Lysacek of the United States battled for gold, surrounded by debate over whether the men's event was an event at all without the quadruple jump.

Throughout the 2010 Olympics, audiences were treated to personal-best performances even as the difficulty level of many of the programs went beyond what had been seen in past competitions. From a fan's point of view—whether you were a casual viewer, an occasional enthusiast, or a long-time figure skating aficionado—the whole experience was fresh. The innovative performances, the execution of the elements, the transitional movements, even the commentary from the media had all changed. We had clearly entered a new era of figure skating.

What drove these new developments? Why did we witness such an evolution in a well-loved sport so seemingly steeped in tradition? Many of the changes were natural—a new generation of skaters who, like all athletes, were pushing the physical and creative boundaries of their sport. But the single biggest change was the new judging system for international figure skating competitions. The judges in Vancouver and, shortly after, at the World Championships in Turin, Italy, were working within a new system that had been in development since the 2002 Winter Olympics in Salt Lake City. This system was adopted officially in 2004 for international events and was used for the first time at an Olympics in Turin, in 2006. The skaters, coaches, and choreographers in Vancouver had designed the skating programs in response to an evolving and complex system of evaluation and points.

The new system of judging worked well. The skaters who won did so by putting down the best performances, the competition was challenging and fair, and the playing field was level. Former champions bit the dust while new heroes were crowned. Overall, the world was treated to one of the most spectacular series of skating performances ever witnessed, with breathtaking artistry and outstanding athleticism that kept fans on the edges of their seats.

left Yu-Na Kim of South Korea won gold at the 2010 Olympics with pure athleticism and elegance, finishing an astonishing 23 points ahead of her nearest competitor. Here she performs a transitional move designed to enhance her music and choreography.

THE EVOLUTION OF
FIGURE SKATING

IGURE SKATING has been an Olympic event since 1908, although the International Skating Union (ISU) was founded in 1892 and international competitions were being held as early as 1860. The system for scoring skaters was developed over many decades.

The Old World of Figure Skating: Nagano and Salt Lake City

For most of the twentieth century, the ISU used a system that became known simply as "6.0"—a reference to the highest possible score that a skater or a team could achieve in a single event.

Under 6.0 there was one panel of nine judges, each representing a different country, who ranked entire performances on a comparative basis. If there were thirty skaters in an event, the judges' task was to rank all thirty in order, from first to last. That also meant that judges were required to remember everything about all thirty performances. Who performed the best jumps? Who was the best spinner? Who had the best footwork? Who was most in sync with the music? Who performed best overall? The judges were then required to balance every consideration and determine a ranking. While it was often obvious who should be in the top and bottom groups, it was sometimes not so clear who should be ranked where in the middle levels. And while rankings were meant to be based on both technical elements and artistry, the reality was that the skater with the best jumps usually surfaced as the winner.

Not only was the 6.0 system of judging subjective and therefore open to criticism, it was also—in the wrong hands—open to manipulation and foul play. This problem became clear during the Ice Dance event at the 1998 Nagano Olympics, when the skill level on the ice was not always accurately reflected in the marking. Rumors of "bloc judging," in which judges were convinced to adjust their scores to favor or punish a particular country's skaters, were rampant. At Nagano, this so-called bloc judging caused Canadian ice dancers Shae-Lynn Bourne and Victor Kraatz to be excluded from the medals, despite their stellar performance on the ice.

The issue of unfair judging reared its head again at the next Winter Olympics, the 2002 Games in Salt Lake City. A scoring scandal rocked the Pair event when Jamie Salé and David Pelletier, another Canadian team, were awarded silver for what many thought was clearly a gold-medal performance. Fans were up in arms, and the North American press blew the issue wide open. As a result of the controversy, and after an investigation into the judging process, a second gold medal for that event was awarded to Salé and Pelletier.

Clearly the ISU needed to turn its attention to the judging process. Something had to be done to regain credibility for the sport and to make competitions fair for the athletes. Skaters needed to be able to compete on a level playing field, and to have the focus turned back on them and their skating, where it should have always been. A new system of judging was developed, and in 2004 the ISU introduced this new scoring program for all international competitions. Since it was launched, the ISU Judging System (ISUJS) has been enhanced and strengthened, and is one of the key elements driving today's new world of figure skating.

The New World of Figure Skating: From 6.0 to Vancouver 2010

The ISU made meaningful changes with the introduction of the ISU Judging System. The changes have not only altered the way judges do their work and how skaters train and perform, but the entire figure skating system, including coaching and choreography. The international competitions in 2010 were opportunities to

right Evan Lysacek of the United States won gold at the 2010 Olympics through sheer determination and hard work. His programs were strategic in design, and he performed with total commitment.

witness the accomplishments and skills of the young skaters who have grown up under this new system, and the results were nothing short of spectacular.

What's new about the new system? Most simply, the ISUJS was developed with a set of objective and measurable criteria, with a series of checks and balances that ensures each well-performed element of a skating performance is rewarded. As well, two panels—a Technical Panel and a Judging Panel—assess the skaters and rate their performances against set criteria and standards.

The Technical Panel assigns the level of difficulty for each performed element. Difficulty levels from 1 (lowest) to 4 (highest) are predetermined by the ISU for specific elements in each of the four categories: Men, Ladies, Dance, and Pairs.

The three members of the Technical Panel—a Technical Controller, a Technical Specialist, and an Assistant Technical Specialist—identify *what* the skaters do; they are not assessing how well the skaters perform. Each level of difficulty for each element has a base point value attached to it, and the point levels are clearly spelled out in an ISU Communication at the start of each competitive season. Officials, coaches, and skaters review this directive, and it becomes the guideline for the Technical Panel to follow when assessing the level of difficulty of each element.

The Judging Panel, which usually consists of nine judges and a referee, who is responsible for the judges and the event logistics on the ice, pays attention to how well the skaters skate. Their job is to assess the *quality* of the execution of each element performed. The judges assign Grade of Execution (GOE) scores for each element based on a scale ranging from -3 to zero to +3. The average GOE score is added by the computer to the base value of the element for a Total Element Score (TES).

The Judging Panel also rates five specific components—Skating Skills, Transitions and Linking Movements, Performance and Execution, Choreography, and Interpretation—on a 10-point scale. The component scores, once averaged and factored by relative importance based on a predetermined ISU scale, are added together to achieve a Total Component Score (TCS).

For both the GOE and the component scores, the highest and lowest of the judges' scores are not counted. The remaining scores are averaged to determine the final element score and final component score. In the end, a skater's total score is the sum of the element score (TES) and the component score (TCS), less any deductions for falls, illegal elements, or time violations.

It sounds complicated—and it is. But it is intentionally so, in order to achieve the ISU's goal of adhering to a clean, measurable adjudication system, thereby ensuring that figure skating remains a respected sport.

The Impact of the ISU Judging System

The ISUJS is based on an accumulation of points—the more points the better. Skaters try to reach the highest level of difficulty for each element in order to achieve the greatest number of points. They pay attention to specific elements like spins and step sequences, which today bear no resemblance to the simpler formats of even five years ago. Spins also have variations that were not attempted before. Lifts have complicated and often risky entries and exits. Ice Dance twizzles—one-foot rotations with which the skater moves across the ice surface— have become fast and furious, with different arm and leg positions.

From a skater's perspective, the new system is far more accurate in its assessment and far more detailed in its feedback. At the end of an event, the skaters receive a summary of their performance that reveals exactly what level of difficulty they achieved, what GOE was assigned for each element, and the scores for each component. Skaters can clearly see where they gained or lost points, where their strengths are, and what they can improve on in for future competitions. Never before have skaters received such concrete and detailed feedback. Being able to measure personal-best performances is refreshing, and the pursuit of excellence is a positive motivator.

This system also allows for more movement among skaters within an event. The 6.0 system (unintentionally) favored skaters and teams who had a reputation or a track record from earlier competitions, since judges could not help but be influenced by previous accomplishments. Today, new skaters and young teams can move ahead quickly based solely on skating ability—which is how it should be. The technical aspects are entirely quantifiable. It used to be that if a skater had a poor Short program and finished toward the bottom of the list, it would be impossible to rise to medal contention in the Free program. Not so now. A skater could be sitting in eighth place after the Short program but still only be a few points out of first. If they then skate a solid Free program, depending how their competitors skate, they could surface the winner. The skaters have a real chance to pull up in the rankings.

Such a possibility was evident with Laura Lepistö's surprise Free skate at the 2010 Olympics—a personal best. The Finnish skater placed tenth in the Short

left Laura Lepistö of Finland performs a back outside spiral in her Free Skate at the Olympics. After placing tenth in the Short program, she skated well enough in the Free to place fourth. Under the ISUJS, solid performances are rewarded regardless of previous placements.

program but skated well enough in the Free program to reach fourth, and claim sixth overall. This upward movement would not likely have happened under the old system of judging.

Most elite skaters are in favor of the new system. They recognize the importance of a level playing field and appreciate that reputation and time served in the sport no longer play a significant role: a relative unknown can rise to the top if the skating is deserving. At the 2010 ISU World Championships in Turin, Mirai Nagasu of the United States won the Short program—ahead of the Olympic gold and silver medalists—in her first World Championship appearance. Her superb skate was rewarded, and her scores were based on what happened on the ice, regardless of previous placement or her reputation.

Parents of young competitive skaters are also in favor of the new system. Parents, of course, are the backbone of support for developing skaters, often altering their own lives to facilitate a child's dream. Certainly they provide the wallet to fund their child's pursuit. When they put their children into an education system, they logically expect some reporting on the child's progress. Under the 6.0 system, there was no accurate, systemized method for providing such feedback. Parents appreciate the ISUJS because young skaters receive performance scorecards immediately after an event is finished, so they have a report that is clear in its analysis of their child's strengths and weaknesses and identifies opportunities for focusing on future success.

From a judge's perspective, the new system is an improvement because it is easier to rate elements and components against a set standard and then move on to assess the next performance. Before, judges had to remember each skater's elements and components throughout the whole competition in order to compare and rank the skaters in a reasonable order. It was a more difficult assignment and, as trained as the judges were, it was nearly impossible for the assessments to be as accurate as they are within today's system.

Importantly, the ISUJS is not as open to manipulation as 6.0 was. In the former system, results were based on a majority consensus. With a panel of nine judges, in order to win a skater needed five judges to place them first. The remaining four judges could place them tenth, seventeenth, third, or eighth—it didn't matter. If the majority of the panel placed a skater first, that skater would win. It was possible—not easy, but possible—to have five judges agree to "vote" the same way and to determine the outcome.

While today's system is not perfect, that kind of manipulation is difficult. A computer randomly selects which seven scores from the nine-judge panel will count, the high and low scores for each element and component are thrown out, and the remaining five scores are averaged. It is not an easy system to manipulate.

Critics of the current system argue that the sport has lost its creativity and that the elements all look the same. Some would like to see more options for achieving the difficult levels. It is true that in the search for greater levels of difficulty, skaters can end up performing the same elements in the same way. Each year, the ISU rules specify which elements will get which level of difficulty, and skaters may simply pick how best to gain those points. The better skaters, however, are discovering new ways to add difficult variations, explore unique position changes within lifts, use innovative footwork, and so on. As they become comfortable with the demands of the elements, they are finding ways to be creative within them.

Some skaters have expressed the desire for more room to develop a story within their programs. One skater has said that choreographing a program today is more like putting together pieces of a puzzle than creating a piece of art. To achieve the difficult levels, step sequences and spins take more time, which doesn't leave much room for a narrative. But that will come as skaters find ways to develop the story within the elements themselves.

Other skaters feel there are not enough points given for the execution of specific difficult elements—a quadruple jump, for example—but as the sport continues to develop, the ISU will review points awarded for different elements to ensure that there is a proper weighting based on difficulty and risk. However, it is accurate to say that jumps alone no longer determine the outcome, and that fully balanced programs are surfacing—ones with well-performed spins and step sequences, notable entrances and exits for jumps, and impressive transitions. Interestingly, the ability to responsively interpret and skate to the music, instead of using it as mere background, is given more prominence under the new system.

Perhaps the biggest criticism of the ISUJS is that the scores are anonymous; some worry that there is no accountability. The ISU purposely decided to make the judges anonymous so they would not be subject to pressure from their own federations to vote a particular way. In the past, that was not uncommon for some countries. Those judges can now judge an event as they see it without fear of recrimination.

In addition, judging anonymously does not mean there is no accountability. There is an ISU Officials Assessment Committee whose role is to monitor and assess the judging and watch for anomalies within it. In some countries—Canada, for instance—the competitions are not judged anonymously, and internationally, the ISU Junior events are not anonymous. Either way, the judging process is the same and carries the same accountability. However, it is no longer the focus of public attention. The skating is.

Is the judging system still evolving? Definitely yes, and the sport of figure skating will continue to evolve in response.

. . . . .

THE ISU JUDGING
SYSTEM

. . . . .

THE ISU Judging System is made up of two distinct but related parts: Technical Elements and Program Components. Under 6.0, two marks were given for a whole performance: one was for Technical Merit, reflecting all the technical elements as a unit, and the other was for Artistic Impression, being the overall impact of the artistry. Under the ISUJS, marks or scores are given for every technical element individually and for five different components reflecting the artistry. As one Olympic judge has so eloquently explained, 6.0 was analogous to typing with two fingers. ISUJS is like typing with ten fingers. You have more to work with.

Technical Elements

The Technical Elements are specific moves that are required of the athletes in each of the Short and Free programs within each discipline. They can change from year to year; the ISU sets the Technical Element requirements annually. Pairs, Single skating, and Ice Dance have required elements distinct to each discipline. For example, Pair teams and Single skaters must do spiral sequences, whereas Ice Dancers do not. Ice Dancers perform a series of Sequential Twizzles as a required element, but Pair teams and Single skaters do not. They might do individual twizzles in their step sequences, but they are usually not in series and are not a specified, required element on their own.

PAIRS

In Pair skating, two people skate in unison, often appearing to skate as one. The more experienced teams seem to have a sixth sense, as each partner knows exactly where the other is at all times. Connections are natural, not labored, and the partners skate close together. Some people confuse Pairs and Ice Dance, although there are significant differences between the two disciplines. For example, in Pairs the man lifts the woman above his head with fully extended arms; in Dance, the lifts are not done with arms fully extended above the head. Pair teams do required jumps and throws; Dance teams do not. The technical elements for Pair teams have become more difficult under the ISUJS.

Pair Lifts Driven by the quest for points, Pair teams today are performing more complicated lifts and striving for the highest level of difficulty. Instead of simple entries and exits, teams are performing difficult variations on take-offs and landings. Examples include the somersault or spread eagle entry or exit, the one-hand take-off or landing, or a dance lift moving immediately into the Pair lift with the woman not having ice contact in between. Once the lift is fully elevated, other difficult features can be introduced, for example a one-arm hold by the man, a change of hold during the rotation while the woman is still in the air, or the woman moving a leg, arm, or her upper body in such a way that affects her balance, which makes the position difficult to maintain.

Some lifts incorporate a "carry," in which the man stops the rotation of the lift and—with the woman suspended for at least three seconds—performs crossovers, skates on one foot, does a spread eagle, or performs some other difficult move. It's even harder to change the direction of rotation within the lift—it is not seen often, but some teams have the required control and balance. Like all of the lift variations, these moves require great flexibility and strength.

Death Spirals The Death Spiral is a difficult but compulsory element in which the man pivots on one skate while the woman, who is holding his hand, circles

below Yuko Kavaguti and Alexander Smirnov of Russia perform a "carry" within their lift in their Free program at the 2010 Olympics. Smirnov balances on one foot once he stops the rotation, a difficult feature. Kavaguti's position is considered difficult as it affects her core balance.

around him with her body nearly parallel to the ice. She can be facing forward or backward, and be on her inside or outside edge. To achieve maximum points, the woman should be as low as possible, and her body should be horizontal. The level of difficulty can be increased by performing a challenging entry into the Death Spiral that affects core balance, holding a difficult position within the Death Spiral, or including a challenging exit, such as an immediate transition into a lift or jump.

The man must stay in a deep pivot position for at least one full revolution. Each additional revolution in this low position will be counted as a feature as many times as it is repeated. Consequently, Death Spirals today often have two or three revolutions; a few years ago, one full revolution was sufficient.

At the 2010 Olympics, China's Qing Pang and Jian Tong included a back outside Death Spiral in both their Short and Free programs, but both times it was graded only Level 1. None of their difficult features counted because Qing was not in a low enough position for at least one revolution. By the time they reached the Worlds, they had fixed this problem and were awarded Levels 3 and 4 for their Death Spiral.

above Qing Pang and Jian Tong of China perform their back outside Death Spiral at the Worlds in Turin. Pang's body is low enough—her head is below her skating knee—to achieve a high level of difficulty. Tong's deep pivot position is excellent. Pang's holding of her free foot is a difficult feature.

Amanda Evora and Mark Ladwig of the United States perform side by side solo spins in a sit position. Holding the free foot is considered a difficult feature. They are spinning in unison but may have improved their GOE mark if they had spun closer together.

Pair Side by Side Solo Spins Side by side solo spins for Pair teams include many variations and take much longer to perform than in previous years. A common solo spin five years ago might have been a camel spin, followed by a sit spin, with a change to the other foot to perform a back sit spin. The full spin might take ten seconds. Today this spin could take twice that time, in order to achieve all of the necessary features. For example, each feature needs to be performed for a minimum of two revolutions to be counted. To ensure that this happens, the skaters will often do three revolutions, which adds even more time. To be counted as a difficult spin variation there must be a change in position or movement of a leg, an arm, a hand, or the head that requires physical strength or flexibility and that has an effect on core balance. And, of course, these spins are to be done with speed, in full unison, and as close together as possible.

Pair Spin Combinations The Pair spin combination, in which the skaters spin around the same axis while maintaining contact with each other, has also developed under the current system. In the past, teams would spin in two basic positions. Now they spin in three basic positions with difficult variations. Again, the quest is on for challenging features ranging from difficult variations in position, to spinning in both directions, to spinning with six or more revolutions in one position. Like many of the other elements, these spins take more time to perform than in the past, and skaters' spinning ability has greatly improved.

Step Sequences Step sequences in Pairs consist of a variety of complex steps and turns designed to use the full ice surface. They take much longer than and bear little resemblance to the sequences performed at the 2002 Salt Lake City Olympics. At those Games, China's Xue Shen and Hongbo Zhao performed a straight line step sequence in their Short program that took nine seconds. By contrast, Germany's Aliona Savchenko and Robin Szolkowy's straight line step sequence in their Short program at the 2010 European Championships took twenty-three seconds, more than twice as long. Why? In 2002, no specific footwork requirements existed. Step sequences were driven by the music and where the sequence fell in the program, and unless the sequence was brilliant or unique, the judges often just marked that the element was done.

Today it's more complicated. To achieve the greatest points, Pair teams must include four of five possible footwork features, including a variety of turns and steps by both partners, body rotations on the turns and steps in either direction, full use of upper body movement, changes of position for at least one-third of the sequence, and steps and turns while in contact with each other. The turns can include three turns, twizzles, brackets, loops, counters, and rockers, and the steps can include toe steps, chassés, mohawks, choctaws, cross rolls, running steps, and curves with change of edges. These footwork features are challenging to choreograph, energy draining to perform, and take up more of the allotted performance time.

Not many Pair teams have achieved a perfect Level 4 in their step sequences—at the 2010 Olympics, not one team reached the top level. At the 2010 Worlds, only Qing Pang and Jian Tong of China, the eventual winners, achieved Level 4 in their straight line step sequence in the Short program. Why is it so difficult? Not only must the skaters perform the turns, steps, rotations, and body movements, but these movements must be done cleanly and be clearly identifiable.

below Anabelle Langlois and Cody Hay of Canada perform a Pair Spin Combination at the Olympics. Both are in full sit position with their skating thighs parallel to the ice. Anabelle's free leg is held to the back, and Cody's free leg is out to the side—both difficult features.

SINGLES

As in Pairs, for Singles the ISU clearly spells out at the start of each competitive season what elements and variations will achieve maximum point levels. The Short program has eight required elements—three jump elements, three different spins, and two step sequences. The Free program is similar for spins and step sequences and there is a maximum number of jump elements: eight for Mens and seven for Ladies, one of which must be an axel-type jump.

Jumps Jumps have always been a key part of Single events, and under the new system the jump elements themselves have not changed: a lutz is still a lutz, an axel is still an axel. But today, the Technical Panel carefully assesses whether the skaters achieve full rotation; if they don't, the jumps are downgraded. At the 2010 Olympics, a triple flip that was rotated less than 2¾ turns was downgraded to a double flip. The base value of the jump dropped from 5.5 to 1.7 points. For the 2011 competitive season, the ISU is proposing that a downgrade will happen if the triple is performed with less than 2½ rotations. These fine details are easy for the audience to miss.

If a skater intends to launch from a particular edge but changes the edge before take-off, the Technical Panel still calls it the intended jump and awards the point value of the intended jump, but sends a message to the judge's screens reflecting the change of take-off edge. The GOE score will be negatively affected.

In the past, judges may or may not have caught take-off or rotation errors. It often depended upon where on the panel a judge sat and their line of observation. When "in doubt," judges were instructed to rule in favor of the skater. With only one mark given for all of the technical elements in a program, such errors might not have had much bearing on the final score. Now, all judges are alerted to these errors and are obliged to reflect them in their scoring. Those who perform the jumps with full rotation and clean and proper take-off edges are rewarded for doing so, while those who do not are penalized.

Some who watched the 2010 Men's Olympic Free Skate program thought that American Johnny Weir had

below Kevin van der Perren of Belgium performs a difficult feature with his arms extended above his head as he spins in a full sit position. The buttocks must be below the skating knee, with the thigh of the skating leg parallel to the ice.

been under-marked for what appeared to be a near-flawless performance. However, it wasn't apparent to the audience that for his first jump—a triple flip—he changed his take-off edge from the correct inside edge to the incorrect outside edge, obliging the judges to give him negative GOE scores. A jump that appeared to the audience to be strong in fact cost him points.

Jumps that are fully rotated, launched from the correct edge, and executed well are rewarded in the GOE scores. Yu-Na Kim of South Korea's jump combination in the Olympic Short program was a triple lutz triple toe loop. It was so well done she earned 12.00 points on that element alone. By contrast, Japan's Miki Ando, the world champion in 2007, suffered a downgrade in her Olympic Short program for her triple lutz triple loop jump combination because she did not have full rotation on the triple loop. The base value of the combination went from 11.00 to 7.50 points. She also put her free foot down after the loop jump, so she received further negative GOE scores for a total of only 6.30 points, for what was meant to be a high-scoring combination.

Spins Under the 6.0 system, little attention was paid to spins unless a skater was particularly adept. It was frustrating to judge a skater like Switzerland's Lucinda Ruh, who had brilliant spins with athletic positions and fast, multiple rotations, yet could never win because her jumps were not strong. Not enough credit was given to spectacular spinners.

As in Pairs, individual skaters have numerous options for increasing the level of difficulty in spins. These movements can be done in the basic camel, sit, or

upright positions, or while changing between them. For example, a skater might do a sit position with hands clasped behind the back and then draw them upward above the head; or a skater could move into a Biellman while spinning in an upright position. These features require strength and flexibility and affect spinning balance.

Increasing the speed within the spin adds a difficult feature, as does inserting a jump in which the skater jumps up cleanly, lands on the same foot, and continues spinning. To encourage more revolutions, points are awarded if skaters spin for at least eight revolutions without a change of position, foot, or edge—the faster the better. It can be lovely to watch. As in Pairs, skaters can spin on both edges with at least two revolutions on each edge, in the same basic position. In the 2010 competitive season, a well-performed Level 4 spin combination with a change of foot and position (+2 GOE) could net the same points as an average-scored triple salchow jump (0 GOE).

Stéphane Lambiel of Switzerland is a skater who pays attention to spins. They were the best parts of his 2010 Olympic programs. He spins furiously fast with exciting body positions and variations. His last spin in his Olympic Free program—a change foot combination—earned +3 GOE scores from every judge.

Spiral Sequences The spiral sequence is a required element in women's Short and Free programs, but not in men's. The men can perform a spiral, and many do it well, but it is not a required element. For women, however, the spiral sequence is an opportunity to showcase the beauty of figure skating.

Under 6.0 judging, a spiral within a sequence had no specific time duration. Now it must be held for at least three seconds. As well, three different spirals must be included in a single sequence, each held for three or more seconds, and with a change of foot within the sequence. The spiral sequence can be any combination of curves—a serpentine design, a circle, or a combination of both patterns, as long as it uses the full ice surface.

To achieve an increased level of difficulty within the spiral sequence, several things can be done. A common move is to change the edge within a spiral, with a three-second hold of each edge before and after the change. Variations of position that affect core balance also qualify as difficult features, such as lifting the free leg forward and in front of the skating leg, twisting the upper body, or skating in a Biellman position, with one foot held above and behind the skater's head.

Michelle Kwan of the United States was the queen of spiral sequences in her era. Her forward inside spiral that changed to a forward outside spiral was breathtaking. As a judge, it gave me goosebumps. Her edges were strong and her spiral position was exquisite. Fellow American Sasha Cohen was also brilliant with her spiral extension. In competition—Kwan from 1994 to 2003 and Cohen from 2002 to 2006—and later in shows, these two skaters set a standard for spirals that many still aspire to.

Step Sequences Women and men have different requirements for step sequences. Men perform two different step sequences in both the Short and Free programs, while women perform one step sequence in each in addition to the spiral sequence. The step sequences can follow a circular pattern using the full width of the ice surface, a serpentine pattern with at least two bold curves from one end of the ice to the other, or a straight line pattern, usually skated from corner to corner of the ice surface or straight down its middle.

To achieve the highest level of difficulty, the skater must perform four challenging features, including at least five different turns and three different steps, all executed at least once in both directions. "Both directions" refers to rotational direction, to the left or to the right. The step sequences are tricky to execute and complex to choreograph. In addition, skaters do full-body rotations in each

far left In her Olympic Short program, Mao Asada of Japan shows flexibility by performing a left forward inside spiral with a Biellman position—a difficult feature. She earned Level 4 difficulty for her spiral sequence and two additional GOE points above base value for her spiral positions.

left American Michelle Kwan's spirals are still aspired to by other skaters, even seven years after she retired from competition. She always exuded joy during her spiral sequences, which were choreographed to enhance the musical composition of the program.

above Daisuke Takahashi of Japan performed brilliant step sequences in his Free program at the 2010 Olympics. He captured the musical nuances, and his steps and turns were crisp with quick changes of direction, gaining points that helped offset mistakes in his jump elements.

direction for at least one-third of the pattern, must demonstrate full upper-body movement—meaning with the arms, head, and torso—and have quick changes of rotational direction.

In today's system, step sequences take more time, are more intricate, contain better edges, and include a greater variety of turns. Skaters also pay more attention to the music, and choreographers ensure that step sequences match the music's phrasing.

As an example, Mao Asada of Japan's best element in her Short program at the 2010 Olympics was her straight line step sequence. It was filled with highlights and intricate steps that expressed the music well. She seemed to come alive within it. In her Olympic Short program, Rachael Flatt from the United States performed an entertaining straight line step sequence with a saucy interpretation of the music. Joannie Rochette from Canada earned good points on her straight line step sequence in her Short program because her steps, turns, and body movements connected to and matched her tango music.

In the Men's event at the 2010 Olympics, Daisuke Takahashi of Japan performed brilliant step sequences in his Free program. They were intricate, quick, and highlighted the musical nuances. Evan Lysacek of the United States was able to gain points on Russia's Evgeni Plushenko with his well-choreographed and well-executed step sequences in both his Short and Free programs. Step sequences carry more weight under ISUJS than they did under the 6.0 judging system.

ICE DANCE

Ice Dance has exploded onto the athletic stage. It has always been considered a sport, but it didn't always have quantifiable criteria. Now, specified elements within Ice Dance are tangible and measurable, and the degree of fitness needed to perform the difficult elements is exceptional.

In the 1980s, Jayne Torvill and Christopher Dean were icons of Ice Dance with their brilliant thematic programs, but the sport has grown so much since then. The current Olympic and world champions, Canadians Tessa Virtue and Scott Moir, along with Americans Meryl Davis and Charlie White, Olympic and

world silver medalists, have pushed Ice Dance in new directions. The performances are more risky, more intricate, and much more difficult. These two teams are leading the way, and rising to the challenges presented by the new judging system.

Ice Dance has consisted of three programs—the Compulsory Dance, Original Dance, and Free Dance—but at the ISU Congress in June, 2010, a proposal was passed to drop Compulsory and Original Dance and to introduce a combined Short Dance to replace both. This means that the 2010 Olympics and World Championships were the last events at which a Compulsory Dance was skated in competition at this level. Ice Dance will become a two-part event in the future, similar to the other disciplines. As with the entire sport of figure skating, Ice Dance continues to evolve.

Dance Lifts Most dance teams at an international level attempt lifts with the highest level of difficulty, as set out in the current year's ISU Communications. Under 6.0, difficulty within a lift was not defined or measured. Today it is. A

top left In their Olympic Free program, Oksana Domnina and Maxim Shabalin of Russia perform a curve lift with Domnina in a full split position and Shabalin skating an inside spread eagle—both difficult features, as they were held for three seconds.

top right At the Olympics, Jana Khokhlova and Sergei Novitski of Russia perform a rotational lift in which Novitski rotates several times holding Khokhlova with only one arm, which is considered a difficult feature.

Level 4 dance lift must be difficult for both the lifting and the lifted partner. Usually the lifting partner is the man, but that's not always the case as teams become more creative.

Lifts have strict time limits. A short lift—stationary, straight line, curve, or rotational—can be a maximum of six seconds, while a long lift—a serpentine, reverse rotational, or combination—can last a maximum of twelve seconds. One of the duties of the referee on the Judging Panel for Ice Dance is to time the lifts. The skaters have a mandatory deduction for each lift exceeding the limit. Six seconds is not a lot of time within which to perform creative and difficult entries and exits, along with the changes of position within the lifts. In close competitions, extended lift deductions can affect placement. Virtue and Moir placed second to Davis and White in the Free Dance at the 2010 World Championships because of an extended lift deduction on their now famous "Canada Goose" lift.

What makes a dance lift difficult? For the lifting partner, examples would be sustaining a challenging position for at least three seconds, moving through a specified number of rotations, or lifting, holding, and setting down the partner with one hand only. For the lifted partner, difficulty could mean sustaining a difficult pose for at least three seconds, or for a specified number of rotations, or moving through a significant change of pose during the lift. A creative or difficult entry—perhaps an unexpected entry without any lead-up or a transitional movement by the lifted partner—can also upgrade a lift to a higher level.

The Judging Panel has clear guidelines for marking lifts regarding their fit with the character and phrasing of the music. If the lift does not match the musical phrasing, the GOE score must be negative, even if the lift itself is well performed. As well, if the music is a tango, a flowing, waltz-like lift would not be an appropriate reflection of the character of the music and the GOE would have to be lowered. Consequently, today we see lifts that enhance the choreography because they fit the musical rhythm and reflect the character of the chosen dance.

Synchronized Twizzles A notable Ice Dance coach says that Ice Dance twizzles—one-foot rotations with which the skaters move across the ice surface—have become like the triple axels in Single skating. While a small mistake in a spin or a lift can sometimes be camouflaged, an error in a twizzle is obvious. Twizzles were always included in dance programs but not often performed in a series, back to back, or with as many revolutions as they are today. Now, Synchronized Twizzles

right Meryl Davis and Charlie White of the United States showcase their spectacular twizzles in the Original Dance at the 2010 Worlds. They rotate closely together with speed and with difficult features: one arm above the head and the other grasping the blade of the free leg.

is a specified element in both the Original Dance and the Free Dance.

There are four types of twizzles, defined by their entry edge: Forward Inside, Forward Outside, Backward Inside, and Backward Outside. For Level 4 difficulty, each twizzle in the series must have a different entry edge and a different direction of rotation, and skaters must do at least four rotations in each twizzle with a change of foot or step in between. Skaters can take only one step between twizzles in the Original Dance and up to three steps between them in the Free Dance. Both partners must perform three additional features within the twizzles, such as upper body and hand moves or skating leg and free leg features.

The best skaters will perform the twizzles close together and in perfect unison, and the speed of rotation sets the best teams apart. The top teams today are doing up to six rotations in each twizzle and rotating furiously.

At the 2010 Olympics and World Championships, the fastest twizzles were performed by Meryl Davis and Charlie White. They approach twizzles with speed, have no hesitation on the entry, and perform multiple rotations rapidly, in close proximity, and with perfect unison.

Dance Spins Spins have become a required element within the Free Dance, and Ice Dancers have risen to the challenge. It is not uncommon to see dancers masterfully spin in both directions—which is considered a difficult feature.

Dancers perform either a Dance Spin—with at least six full rotations for Level 4 without a change of foot—or a Combination Spin that has a change of foot and at least three full rotations on each foot. As well, there are complicated requirements for difficult positions within each of the three basic spinning positions—camel, sit, and upright—that are similar to the spin requirements in Pairs and Singles.

above Canada's Vanessa Crone and Paul Poirier practice their spin combination for the Free Dance at the 2010 Worlds. They changed feet to spin in both directions and had beautiful positions and continual speed, earning Level 4 difficulty.

Step Sequences The Ice Dance event includes two types of footwork sequences: a step sequence performed by both skaters in a dance hold, and a step sequence performed separately, with the skaters not touching. The pattern of the sequence in a dance hold must fully use the ice surface and can move in a straight line or in a circular or serpentine design. The not-touching step sequence travels down the center of the ice and is featured only in the Original Dance (now Short Dance) program. It may include mirror or matching footwork, and the partners should skate as closely together as possible without touching.

Each level of difficulty has specifications on dance holds, turns, one-foot skating sections, and additional features like toe steps. Ice dancers focus much of their training on footwork sequences because strategically these moves can make a difference in points. Many teams can achieve Level 4 in lifts, spins, and twizzles, but very few can achieve that highest level of difficulty in step sequences. It can make a difference in close competitions.

Precision and unison of movement is key, and maintaining speed and flow throughout a sequence is challenging. Step sequences are complicated and intricate and take control and energy to perform well. Dancers tend to be the best of all skaters at performing clean and accurate edges, turns, and steps within a sequence. Step sequences that are skated to the music are rewarded in the GOE scores, so today's best skaters perform step sequences that match their music's rhythm and character.

Program Components

Subjectivity is unavoidable in any judged sport. In figure skating, Program Components is the most subjective area. Components covers what was called Artistic Impression under the 6.0 system, but breaks it down into multiple parts. It includes everything in a program outside of the elements. Components are marked on a ten-point scale that corresponds to the degree to which the

component is used, ranging from "very poor" to "outstanding." And efforts have been made to ensure there are defined and specific evaluation criteria within each component, to balance subjectivity.

There are five components: Skating Skills, Transitions and Linking Movements, Performance and Execution, Choreography, and Interpretation.

SKATING SKILLS

The Skating Skills component deals with the skaters' basic skating abilities. It includes edge control with balance over the blade, flow over the ice, speed, direction of skating, and sureness in turns, steps, and edges. Skaters with strong *edge control* display a sense of security—they don't wobble over their blades and they have a strong center of gravity and good body alignment. Their edges are deep on curves and are performed with strength—they skate "into" the ice as opposed to "on top" of the ice.

above Americans Tanith Belbin and Benjamin Agosto skated an energetic Moldavian folk dance for their Olympic Original Dance. Their fast and light step sequences were skated with conviction and included toe steps, hops, and movements in character with the music.

Good *flow* means the skater glides readily over the ice and achieves and maintains speed with ease. Skating with good flow looks efficient, easy, and relaxed. The best skaters also use a range of *speed* in their programs, which can add sensitivity and excitement. Weaker skaters are more cautious in their use of speed.

Direction of skating refers to how comfortable the skater is moving in all directions: forward, backward, clockwise, and counterclockwise. The ability to quickly change directions is key. Judges will reward a skater who uses all directions to weave the elements together, rather than traveling in one direction around the ice.

Sureness relates to the skater's confidence of movement when doing turns and steps, and also to whether the turns are scratchy or skated on clean, identifiable edges.

For Pair and Ice Dance teams, the Skating Skills mark will also reflect whether the skaters have equal or unequal skating abilities.

TRANSITIONS AND LINKING MOVEMENTS

The Transitions and Linking Movements component includes the varied footwork, body movements, skating movements, and "non-listed elements" that link the required elements throughout a program. *Footwork* transitions include different steps, turns, and directions of skating. *Body movement* transitions include different arm, head, torso, and leg positions. *Skating movement* transitions include accents such as spread eagles, pivots, spirals, lunges, arabesques, and Ina Bauer moves.

The *non-listed elements* do not have a point value but add to this component score. They include hops, half loop jumps, inside axel jumps, split jumps, stag jumps, falling leaf jumps, ballet jumps, butterfly jumps, and mazurka jumps.

When assigning a score for Transitions and Linking Movements, consideration is given to the variety of transition tools used—does a skater simply do hops between elements or use a range of transition tools? In Pairs and Dance, do they vary the holds between partners or do they always skate in one type of hold? Consideration is also given to the difficulty of the footwork or movements performed. Were the transition tools simple crossovers or challenging steps and turns with the simultaneous use of different body parts?

The intricacy of the movements is also important for this component score. Did they transition immediately into and out of the elements? For example, was a triple axel preceded by a spread eagle before its take-off? Was the landing followed by a special body position or a series of weaving turns and edges on the landing foot? Such moves can add to the complexity of the actual element and make it more interesting. The quality of the transitions is also considered. Are they clean and clear? For Pairs and Dance, are the transitional movements skated in unison?

Skaters are paying more attention to transitions and to linking footwork and movements in response to the adoption of this component score. Under the

below "Non-listed" elements are transitional movements that on their own do not gain points but are factored into the overall Transitions component score. One example is a split jump, which Adam Rippon of the United States performed superbly at the 2010 Worlds.

6.0 system there was no place to reward the skater who attempted difficult and intricate movements between elements. Even today, some skaters—Evgeni Plushenko and Brian Joubert are examples—still openly state that they do not spend a lot of time on transitions; they prefer to focus on jumps. However, a skater who adds effective transitional movements will have a more well-rounded program and will be rewarded in this component. Jeffrey Buttle of Canada won the 2008 World Championships ahead of Joubert without a quadruple jump but with the highest score for Transitions.

PERFORMANCE AND EXECUTION

The Performance and Execution component covers the skaters' involvement in and commitment to the program—the Performance—and the quality and precision of the movements within the performance—the Execution. "Involvement" means that the skaters appear intellectually involved: they understand the music and the message they are trying to convey, rather than just skating steps assigned by the choreographer. As well, the skaters must be physically involved—each movement

should have a sensible purpose. Finally, judges must determine whether the skaters are emotionally involved—do they have an emotional connection with the judges and the audience? Performance also includes projection and expression—can the skaters reflect the emotional aspects of the music?

For Execution marks, the judges pay attention to the carriage of the skaters—is their core body strong and in alignment, allowing fluid movement between the elements? Is their posture aesthetically pleasing? Style, individuality, and personality are also considered here, and the judges look for a combination of personal, artistic, or unique movements that reflect the story being told or that simply enhance the beauty or distinctiveness of the program.

Clarity of movement is also considered under Execution. This means that the movements are precise with defined positions. Variety and contrast of movement are important—different tempos and rhythms require varied angles, shapes, and levels of body and blade movements. Different movements add interest, while the repetition of similar movements is boring. In Pairs and Ice Dance, as with other components, unison in movement is a key part of the performance.

The score for Performance and Execution reflects how the skaters, through their movements, connect with the audience. Individual skaters or teams who can draw the audience into their performance will see it reflected in a higher score for this component.

CHOREOGRAPHY

Perhaps the Choreography score should be awarded to the choreographer, not the skater, but the skaters make the choreography come alive. Choreography is defined as the intentional arrangement of movements within a program, with consideration to proportion, space, pattern, structure, and musical phrasing. The programs that have a lasting effect on the audience are those in which the choreography, the music, and the skaters are connected. Jamie Salé and David Pelletier's performance to "Love Story" at the 2002 Salt Lake City Olympics is an excellent example, as is Kurt Browning's "Casablanca" program from 1993. In these and other memorable skates, the skaters shared their story with the audience and the audience was rapt.

There are four key points to the Choreography component: Purpose, Structure and Pattern, Body Design and Dimension, and Movement and Music Phrasing.

In considering Purpose, judges watch for the skaters' movements and elements to correspond to the development of a story or theme, or the interpretation of a musical composition. Is the skater able to use movement as language to express a concept? Do the elements have a purpose and a meaning? For example, at the

top left Americans Emily Samuelson and Evan Bates perform a lovely linking movement during their Free Dance at the 2010 Olympics. This move does not gain points on its own but will enhance the overall component score for Transitions.

top right Passion! Intellectual and emotional involvement is part of the component score for Performance and Execution. Here, Tessa Virtue and Scott Moir of Canada portray total commitment during their flamenco Original Dance at the 2010 Olympics.

2010 Olympics, Yuko Kavaguti and Alexander Smirnov of Russia skated a balletic Short program to "The Swan." She was the white swan and he was the black swan. They floated from element to element with purposeful connecting movements that helped to develop their story.

Structure and Pattern refers to how well the elements and movements are woven together to produce a logical and pleasing pattern on the ice. Is the full ice surface used? Does the program include clockwise and counterclockwise movements, as well as circular and linear movements? A program that rotates generally in one direction, or that focuses its highlights to the judges' side of the rink, is not well choreographed or inclusive of the full audience.

The skater's body is a tool used to create a design or dimension in space. When scoring for Body Design and Dimension, judges take notice if a skater's body movements are mostly upright and so don't occupy expanded space. Skaters who reach out of the upright position and use a full range of motion occupy more space and create greater interest. It is also more demanding, and therefore rewarded in this component score.

Movement and Music Phrasing is a key part of the Choreography score. The music often calls for a particular movement or element to be executed at a precise moment. Skaters must make sure the highlights of the music are matched with appropriate moves. For example, a circular step sequence in a Free Dance will have more impact if it matches the musical phrasing. Tension (or release of tension) in the music can be highlighted with an element or movement that fits with that particular phrasing and reflects the musical energy. The best skaters move in unison with the music.

At the Olympics and the Worlds, the Free Dance performed by Meryl Davis and Charlie White portrayed choreography at its best. They skated to music from *The Phantom of the Opera* and their movements perfectly matched its tension and releases. The music exploded at the start and so did their skating. Their fast twizzles fit its rush. Then, when the music called for it, they readily transitioned from intensity to tenderness.

INTERPRETATION

Interpretation refers to the relationship of the skaters' movements to the style, character, and phrasing of the music. Whereas Choreography is placement driven, meaning it deals with where on the ice surface or where in the musical structure it makes sense to perform a particular element, Interpretation is skater driven, meaning it focuses on how the skater interprets the music. The three key points are Musical Movement, Expressive and Nuanced Movement, and Effortless Movement.

Points for Musical Movement are awarded if the skater is connected to the music rather than merely performing with the music as background, and if the skaters' movements are appropriate to the style, character, and phrasing of the music. Expressive and Nuanced Movement means the skaters use finesse, refinement, and subtlety to reflect the nuances of the music and respond to variations in intensity or tempo. For example, if the music becomes explosive, can the skater perform an explosive movement to capture it? Judges also watch for the appearance of Effortless Movement—does the skater demonstrate a natural ease and fluidity of movement in time to the music and an effortless correspondence to musical changes?

At the 2010 Olympics, Virtue and Moir skated a brilliant Original Dance program to Spanish flamenco music. They were in character throughout—the steps, movements, and hand claps were crisp when the music called for it and tender when the music was more fluid. Virtue flipped her red skirt with great effect to match the musical nuances. The upside-down flip entry into the curved lift matched the musical crescendo. The connection between the skaters and their

far left Body design and dimension in space are considered in the component score for Choreography. At Skate America 2009, Evan Lysacek's creative position showed how skaters can reach out and fully occupy space, initiating interest and enhancing their choreography.

left Matching skating movements to the musical phrasing is a key part of the Choreography score. Meryl Davis and Charlie White of the United States, skating their Free Dance to *The Phantom of the Opera,* captured the musical phrasing with movements that matched what the music called for.

passion for the music was palpable. Their interpretation was genuine and they won the Original Dance with a season's-best point total of 68.41.

At the 2010 World Championships in Turin, Italian ice dancers Federica Faiella and Massimo Scali performed an Italian folk dance as their Original Dance, appealing to their home country. All of their movements were meaningful in Italian culture. Federica dressed in black, indicating that her character had just lost her husband, and in a playful performance, Massimo tried to seduce her for the first part of the dance; she fell in love with him in the second part. They also carried hand clappers and clicked them to the music in authentic interpretation.

The five Program Component scores have caused skaters and their choreographers to pay attention to areas of the programs that they might not have under 6.0. The components reinforce the benefits of designing and skating well-rounded programs. Young skaters today must factor components into their training and focus.

Vancouver 2010: The Men's Battle for Gold— The ISU Judging System in Action

Several serious medal contenders competed in the Men's program at Vancouver's Olympics, including four former world champions: Evgeni Plushenko of Russia, Stéphane Lambiel of Switzerland, Brian Joubert of France, and Evan Lysacek of the United States. As well, there were major new contenders in Patrick Chan of Canada and Japan's Daisuke Takahashi and Nobunari Oda. Plushenko was the reigning men's Olympic champion from Turin in 2006, and had come to these Games to reclaim gold. How the scoring broke down between the gold medal contenders in the Men's event is a perfect example of the ISUJS in action.

Heated discussions went on in private and through the media about whether or not the men should be required to perform a quadruple jump. Plushenko and Joubert asserted that it was not men's figure skating without the quad; they both intended to include one and criticized those skaters who did not. In the end, however, it came down to Plushenko, with his quad, and Lysacek, without.

In the Short program, Plushenko followed his quad toe loop with a triple toe loop. The base value of those two jumps was 13.80, and since they were well executed, he received a total point score for that single element of 14.80—that's huge. In contrast, Evan Lysacek did not include a quad for his combination jump but instead did a triple lutz followed by a triple toe loop. The base value of these two jumps was 10.00, and with the GOE marks combined, the total point value of Lysacek's combination was 11.00. Based on this one element, Lysacek was 3.80 points behind Plushenko.

However, the current judging system is not only about jumps. All elements are important, as are all components. Lysacek earned 6.10 points—2.10 more than Plushenko—on his energetic circular step sequence. Plushenko's circular step sequence was not as difficult, and his point total for that element was 4.00. By excelling at a non-jump element, Lysacek gained ground on Plushenko despite the quad. Plushenko had a Total Element Score of 51.10 to Lysacek's 48.30, a 2.80 difference.

In the Program Component scores, both skaters fared identically on Skating Skills, with 8.20. However, Plushenko lost marks through his lack of attention to Transitions and Linking Movements—his Transitions score was 6.80 while Lysacek's was 7.95, more than a point ahead. Lysacek's scores for Choreography and Interpretation were also higher than Plushenko's, and in the end Lysacek's Total Component Score was 42.00 to Plushenko's 39.75, a 2.25 difference.

When the element scores and the component scores were added together, Lysacek had closed the points gap with a total Short program score of 90.30 to Plushenko's 90.85. Going into the Free program, Lysacek was .55 points behind. The quad—even though it had been well executed—did not give Plushenko a significant edge.

PLUSHENKO AND LYSACEK's match-up became more interesting in the Free skate. What strategy would the men use? They had to consider their individual strengths and weaknesses and their level of conditioning. In the Free skate, a jump element performed after the halfway mark in the program achieves a

left Part of the component score for Interpretation involves the skaters' ability to portray the music's character by reflecting its nuances. In their Original Dance at the Olympics, Federica Faiella and Massimo Scali of Italy interpreted their Italian folk dance with finesse.

below The scorecard for the Men's Free program at the 2010 Olympics shows that Evgeni Plushenko's total base value for all elements before GOE (75.03) was higher than Evan Lysacek's (74.93). However, Lysacek outperformed Plushenko in the quality of execution of the elements, as shown by the judges' GOE scores and Total Element Scores.

JUDGES DETAILS PER SKATER / NOTATION DÉTAILLÉE DES JUGES

THU 18 FEB 2010 / JEU 18 FÉV 2010

Rank	Name				NOC Code	Starting Number	Total Segment Score	Total Element Score	Total Program Component Score (factored)	Total Deductions
1	LYSACEK Evan				USA	19	167.37	84.57	82.80	0.00

#	Executed Elements	Info	Base Value	GOE						The Judges Panel (in random order)				Scores of Panel
1	3Lz+3T		10.00	1.40	2	2	1	2	1	0	1	2	1	11.40
2	3A		8.20	0.60	1	0	0	1	0	0	1	1	1	8.80
3	3S		4.50	1.00	0	2	0	1	1	0	1	1	1	5.50
4	CiSt4		3.90	1.20	2	1	1	2	1	1	1	1	2	5.10
5	FSSp4		3.00	0.80	2	2	2	2	1	1	1	2	2	3.80
6	3A+2T		10.45 x	-0.56	-1	-1	-1	0	0	-1	0	0	-1	9.89
7	3Lo		5.50 x	1.00	1	2	0	1	1	1	1	1	1	6.50
8	3F+2T+2Lo	!	9.13 x	-0.40	0	-1	-1	1	0	-1	-1	0	0	8.73
9	3Lz		6.60 x	1.40	1	2	1	2	1	0	1	2	1	8.00
10	2A		3.85 x	0.80	1	1	0	1	0	0	1	1	1	4.65
11	FCSSp4		3.00	0.50	2	1	0	2	1	0	1	1	1	3.50
12	SlSt3		3.30	0.90	2	2	1	3	1	1	2	2	2	4.20
13	CCoSp4		3.50	1.00	2	0	2	3	2	1	2	2	3	4.50
			74.93											84.57

Program Components	Factor											
Skating Skills	2.00	8.00	7.50	8.75	8.75	8.00	8.25	8.25	8.00	8.50		8.20
Transitions / Linking Footwork	2.00	8.00	7.50	8.50	8.50	8.00	8.00	7.25	8.00	8.25		7.95
Performance / Execution	2.00	8.75	8.75	9.00	9.25	8.50	8.00	8.00	8.75	8.50		8.50
Choreography / Composition	2.00	8.50	8.25	8.75	9.00	8.00	8.25	8.00	8.50	8.75		8.35
Interpretation	2.00	8.50	8.00	9.00	9.25	8.25	8.25	8.25	8.50	8.75		8.40
Judges Total Program Component Score (factored)												82.80
Deductions:												0.00

Rank	Name				NOC Code	Starting Number	Total Segment Score	Total Element Score	Total Program Component Score (factored)	Total Deductions
2	PLUSHENKO Evgeni				RUS	24	165.51	82.71	82.80	0.00

#	Executed Elements	Info	Base Value	GOE						The Judges Panel (in random order)				Scores of Panel
1	4T+3T		13.80	0.80	1	1	1	1	0	-1	1	1	2	14.60
2	3A		8.20	-0.36	0	-1	1	0	-1	-1	-1	0	1	7.84
3	3A+2T		9.50	1.00	1	2	1	1	0	0	2	1	2	10.50
4	3Lo		5.00	0.60	0	0	1	1	-1	0	1	1	1	5.60
5	FSSp3		2.60	0.14	0	0	2	1	-1	-1	2	0	1	2.74
6	3Lz		6.00	0.60	0	1	1	1	0	0	2	0	2	6.60
7	CSSp4		3.00	0.70	1	2	2	1	1	1	2	1	2	3.70
8	CiSt3		3.30	0.80	2	1	3	2	0	2	2	1	2	4.10
9	3Lz+2T		8.03 x	0.00	0	0	1	0	-1	-1	-1	0	1	8.03
10	3S		4.95 x	0.80	1	1	1	1	0	1	1	0	1	5.75
11	2A		3.85 x	1.00	0	1	1	1	0	2	2	1	1	4.85
12	SlSt3		3.30	1.00	2	1	3	3	1	3	2	1	2	4.30
13	CCoSp4		3.50	0.60	1	1	2	1	1	1	2	2	1	4.10
			75.03											82.71

Program Components	Factor											
Skating Skills	2.00	9.00	7.75	9.00	9.00	8.00	7.25	8.00	8.25	9.00		8.40
Transitions / Linking Footwork	2.00	8.75	6.00	8.00	8.75	6.00	6.50	7.25	7.25	8.50		7.25
Performance / Execution	2.00	9.00	9.50	9.50	8.75	8.25	8.00	8.75	8.25	9.25		8.80
Choreography / Composition	2.00	9.25	7.75	9.00	9.00	7.75	7.50	8.50	7.75	8.75		8.20
Interpretation	2.00	9.25	9.50	9.50	9.00	7.50	7.75	8.50	8.00	9.50		8.75
Judges Total Program Component Score (factored)												82.80
Deductions:												0.00

10 percent higher base point value, as skaters are more fatigued. For example, a triple lutz at the beginning of a program has a base value of 6.00. Past the halfway mark, its base value rises to 6.60. Skaters who are fit enough to do difficult jumps and combinations in the latter half of their program are rewarded for their conditioning and for taking risks.

The Free program score sheets for Evan Lysacek and Evgeni Plushenko reveal the new judging system in action. The left side of the sheet lists all of the elements performed—jumps, spins, and step sequences. The base value column shows the base value of each element without any judging scores. The GOE column shows the overall averaged Grade of Execution score awarded by the judges for that element. This is the computer's tabulation of the scores of seven randomly selected judges, with the high and low scores dropped, and the remaining five scores averaged.

The remaining columns show the judges' scores in random order—this indicates the range of scores awarded. The last column on the right shows the total score for each element once the averaged GOE score has been added to the base value. The "x" notation in the base value column indicates jump elements performed after the halfway mark of the program.

top left Evan Lysacek makes the most of every movement. In his Olympic Free program, his spread eagle, a transitional move, was performed with commitment and intensity.

top right Evgeni Plushenko shows confidence and attitude as he attacks his Free program at the Olympics. At the end of his performance he drew an imaginary sword, as if laying down the gauntlet.

Plushenko opened his Free program with a quadruple toe loop followed by a triple toe loop (4T+3T). Even though he was leaning slightly on the landing of the quad, he earned 14.60 points for the combination. By contrast, Lysacek opened with his strongest combination—a triple lutz triple toe loop combination (3Lz+3T). He performed it well and earned 11.40 points. Lysacek needed to gain 3.20 points to catch up to Plushenko.

The score sheet indicates that Lysacek performed five jump elements in the second half of the program, and so received 10 percent more base value for those jumps; Plushenko did three. Taking the triple lutz (3Lz) as an example, notice that Lysacek did it as his ninth element and gained 6.60 as the base value plus a GOE of 1.40, for a total score of 8.00. Plushenko's triple lutz was his sixth element and in the first half of his program, so he only gained a base value of 6.00. With a GOE of 0.60 he was awarded total points of 6.60. Lysacek gained 1.40 points by placing that one jump in the latter half of his program and performing it well. That takes conditioning, as well as a strategic program design.

Both men performed a triple axel (3A) as their second element, with a base value of 8.20. Plushenko's landing was not controlled so he received negative GOE scores and ended up with 7.84. Lysacek's triple axel was landed solidly, earning positive GOE scores for a total of 8.80. In the last element—a change foot combination spin (CCoSp4)—both skaters earned Level 4 difficulty for a base value of 3.50. However, the judges thought more highly of Lysacek's spin—he earned a GOE of 1.00 to Plushenko's 0.60.

Remarkably, both skaters achieved an identical Total Component Score of 82.80. Plushenko had higher scores for Skating Skills, Performance, and Interpretation, while Lysacek's scores were greater for Transitions and Choreography. Lysacek's straight line step sequence near the end of his program and the combination spin were masterfully choreographed to accent the musical crescendos. Netting it out, Lysacek's performance was a full package of athleticism and artistry, even without the quad. While it was a very close competition, he simply outperformed Plushenko. Lysacek scored 167.37 points in the Free skate. Combined with his second-place Short program score, his overall event score was 257.67, earning him the gold medal. Plushenko scored 165.51 in the Free Skate. This, combined with his winning Short program score, earned him the silver medal and an overall score of 256.36.

Highlights from the 2009–2010 Grand Prix Season, the 2010 Olympic Winter Games, and the 2010 ISU World Figure Skating Championships

. . . . .

TRIUMPH ON ICE

. . . . .

{ PAIRS }

left Xue Shen and Hongbo Zhao of China skated a masterful Olympic Short program, earning first place. Here they perform a back outside Death Spiral with Shen holding her free foot—a difficult feature.

below In their Olympic Free program, Shen and Zhao earned a 10.00 for Interpretation. Here they display two difficult features: Zhao rotates the lift with one arm, and Shen holds her free foot, affecting her core balance.

left In this signature lift performed during the Olympic Exhibition Gala, Zhao supports the lift with one arm only, while Shen stretches out fully with no hand hold, both difficult features.

below Shen and Zhao's programs included lovely transitional movements. At the beginning of their Short program, they performed a sequence of interesting moves, creating connection between them and establishing a sensitive mood.

right Shen and Zhao express delight at the end of their Short program. Their opening triple toe loops were in complete unison, their triple twist lift was enormous, and a throw triple loop covered the ice.

far left The audience had goose bumps during Qing Pang and Jian Tong of China's first-place Olympic Free program. Their throw jumps covered enormous ice, and their triple twist lift, seen here, was a highlight.

left This lift by Olympic silver medalists Pang and Tong shows a one-arm hold by Tong while Pang holds her free foot, both difficult features. Pang's assisted cartwheel immediately before the lift added to the difficulty.

below This transitional skating movement was a highlight of Pang and Tong's Short program. It emphasized the nuances of the music and helped to link elements in an elegant manner.

below This starting pose launched an inspired Free program for Pang and Tong at the Worlds. Their highest component score was for Performance and Execution. They won the event becoming world champions.

right In their Short program, Pang and Tong perform a pair spin combination. His free leg is extended to the back and hers to the side, both difficult features in the basic sit position.

below Aliona Savchenko and Robin Szolkowy of Germany skated their Free program to music from *Out of Africa*. They included lovely moments, such as the small dance lift seen here.

right In perfect unison, Savchenko and Szolkowy execute a right outside spiral as part of their Free program spiral sequence. Holding their legs up and out to the side is a difficult feature.

below Savchenko and Szolkowy's highest component mark was for Performance and Execution in their "Send in the Clowns" program. Here they perform a back outside Death Spiral with Savchenko holding her free foot.

right Savchenko and Szolkowy perform a signature move at the Worlds in Turin. He holds an outside spread eagle position while Aliona glides on a beautiful right forward outside edge sprial.

above Russians Yuko Kavaguti and Alexander Smirnov made costly errors during their Olympic Free skate. This forward inside Death Spiral did not count because Kavaguti was not low enough, with her head below the knee of her skating foot.

right Kavaguti and Smirnov skated a balletic Short program to "The Swan"—she was the white swan and he the black. They gracefully floated from element to element as they interpreted the music.

far right Kavaguti and Smirnov perform a lovely transitional movement. Kavaguti is in a spiral, and Alexander skates an outside spread eagle. This program worked well at the Olympics and the Worlds.

left Dan Zhang and Hao Zhang of China perform a transitional movement in their Worlds Free program. Some of their best elements at the Worlds and Olympics were throw jumps, with impressive height and solid landings.

below Anabelle Langlois and Cody Hay of Canada display impressive difficult features within a pair lift. Hay supports the lift with one arm during rotations; Langlois holds her free foot, affecting her core balance.

below Jessica Dubé and Bryce Davison of Canada included this back inside Death Spiral in their sensitive Olympic Free program, displaying Dubé's low position and Davison's deep pivot.

right Skating to *Requiem for a Dream* in their Olympic Short program, Dubé and Davison perform a throw triple loop. Their side by side solo spins, skated closely together, were aesthetically pleasing.

far left Maria Mukhortova and Maxim Trankov of Russia perform a pair spin combination in their Olympic Free program. Trankov holds his free foot in a camel spin; Mukhortova does the same as she spins in a full sit.

left This lift—supported by Trankov's one arm and with Mukhortova's demanding air position—shows two difficult features. They placed seventh at the Olympics and moved up to fourth at the Worlds.

below Mukhortova and Trankov perform a back outside Death Spiral. Mukhortova is not low enough with her head below her skating knee but she gets there. They reach for each other's hand to change their hold.

far left Yu-Na Kim of South Korea performs a lovely transitional body movement as she lands her double axel.

left Kim performs a right back outside spiral during her Olympic Short program. Holding her free foot to the front is considered a difficult feature.

below Kim's Olympic Free program was graceful and skilled. Her jumps were clean and fast, her spins had lovely positions, and her step sequences expressed the music. Her overall score of 150.06 was an Olympic record.

right Kim performs a camel spin during her Olympic Free program. Her upper body rotates from the usual camel position—facing down toward the ice—to be facing upward, considered a difficult feature.

below In her Short program, Kim performs a layback spin that displays her elegant position.

far right Kim thrilled the audience with her Olympic Short program, performed to a James Bond medley. All elements fit the music well and she enjoyed her skate, earning a sport record score of 78.50 points.

left Mao Asada skates a left forward outside spiral as part of her spiral sequence in her Short program at the Olympics. Her flexibility was apparent in her beautiful spiral positions.

below In her Olympic Free skate, Asada of Japan performs her straight line step sequence after successfully completing two triple axel jumps—the only competitor to do so.

right At the Worlds, Asada performs a sit spin showing two difficult features: her free foot is crossed over her skating knee, and her arms are held above her back.

below In her Free program, Asada does an outside spread eagle as a linking movement just before her double axel. This was rewarded with a high component score for Transitions.

far right Asada fully extends her free leg near the end of her spiral sequence during the Short program at Trophée Éric Bompard in Paris.

right Joannie Rochette of Canada performs a left forward outside spiral in her Olympic Short program.

below Rochette displayed admirable courage at the Olympics, performing just two days after her mother's sudden death. She skated brilliantly, and her audience—in the arena and around the world—supported her at every step.

far right Rochette performs a spread eagle transitional movement in her Olympic Free program. She skated a sensitive performance, remarkable under the circumstances, earning Olympic bronze.

right In her Olympic Free program, Mirai Nagasu of the United States performs a superb Biellman position as part of her layback spin. She earned plus-3 GOE scores for her fast rotations and impressive positions.

far right Nagasu performs the first part of her layback spin. Holding her free leg to her head highlights her flexibility. The spin progresses to the Biellman position, as seen on the previous page.

left In her Olympic Short program, Nagasu performs a right forward inside spiral as part of her spiral sequence. Her edge quality and agility shine.

below Rachael Flatt of the United States skates a beautiful outside spread eagle as a transitional movement in her Free Skate. She placed seventh at the Olympics and ninth at the Worlds.

far left Laura Lepistö of Finland won bronze at the 2010 Worlds in Turin. Here, she performs a layback spin during her Short program, pulling her free foot to her head—a difficult feature.

left Cynthia Phaneuf of Canada skated well at the Worlds, placing fifth overall. This transitional movement in her Free program displays commitment to her program and her projection to the audience.

below Phaneuf spins in a full sit position, holding her free foot as a difficult feature—one of three basic positions in her change combination spin. She earned a Level 4 difficulty for this element.

below Carolina Kostner of Italy, 2010 European champion, skates a left forward outside spiral in her Short program. She had a disappointing Olympics but rallied to place sixth at the World Championships.

right Skating before her home crowd in Turin, Kostner performs a transitional movement with impressive body extension during her Free program at the Worlds.

{ SINGLES MEN }

left Emphasizing a change in the music and shift in mood, Evan Lysacek of the United States performs a body transitional movement during his Free program at Skate America.

above In his Olympic gold-medal performance, Lysacek performs a spread eagle as a transitional skating movement.

below This movement by Lysacek in his Olympic Short program demonstrates how he effectively uses his body as a choreographic tool, creating design and dimension in space.

right Skating to "Tango Amore" in his Olympic Free program, Evgeni Plushenko of Russia interprets his music with intensity. He is completely committed to his performance and execution.

below Plushenko reaches out to the audience during his Olympic Free program. You can sense his focus in this transitional body movement.

right Plushenko made a forceful statement with his jump combination—a quadruple toe loop triple toe loop—performing both jumps well in his Olympic Short program.

right In his Olympic Free program, Daisuke Takahashi of Japan performs a back camel spin with a difficult position in which he rotates his upper body to face upward.

below Takahashi spins quickly in a full sit position during his Olympic Short program. He achieved Level 4 difficulty for all three spins in the program.

far right With flow and extension, Takahashi lands a jump during his Olympic Free program. His step sequences were brilliantly intricate and matched to the music. He won bronze at the Olympics and gold at the Worlds.

left Stéphane Lambiel of Switzerland skates a transitional movement in his Olympic Short program. He put his foot down on the landing of his quadruple toe loop combination but his brilliant spins kept him in fifth place.

above Lambiel's position in his flying spin—called a "death drop"—is unusual with his head facing downward. One of the best spinners in the world, he rotates quickly with wonderful variations in position.

right Brian Joubert of France reacts with excitement at the end of his Short program at the Worlds. He'd landed his quadruple toe loop triple toe loop jump combination, which had eluded him at the Olympics.

far right In his Worlds Free program, Joubert performs a lunge skating movement as a transition. He landed both quadruple toe loop attempts. After a disappointing Olympics, Joubert won the bronze medal at the Worlds.

right Johnny Weir of the United States displays a balletic interpretation of "Fallen Angels." His performance was passionate, but he lost points by changing the take-off edge on a jump and losing balance in a spin.

below Weir skates an Ina Bauer—a transitional movement—as an accent in his Free program at the Olympics.

far right Skating to "I Love You, I Hate You," Weir performs for the audience in his Olympic Short program. His triple axel was smooth, gaining plus-GOE points, and his step sequences were passionate and fun.

left Nobunari Oda of Japan skated a delightful interpretation of a Charlie Chaplin medley for his Olympic Free program. His skate lace broke, earning a 2.0 deduction—equipment problems are considered the skater's fault.

below Oda performs an expressive transitional movement in his Short program at the Worlds. While jumps eluded him there, he started the season by winning the Trophée Éric Bompard in Paris.

below Sergei Voronov of Russia performs a ballet jump at the Worlds—a transitional "non-listed" element. Points are not gained for this jump, but it's considered in the component score for Transitions and Linking Movements.

right Takahiko Kozuka of Japan skates an outside spread eagle as a linking movement in his Short program at the Worlds. He performs this move well and includes it often in his programs.

above Florent Amodio of France performs a stag jump at the 2010 Olympics. Amodio uses this "non-listed" element effectively as a linking movement—it is considered in the component score for Transitions.

right Tomáš Verner of the Czech Republic displays a fun transitional movement in his Short program at the 2009 Grand Prix in Paris. He uses his music well and is skilled at interpreting its highlights.

{ ICE DANCE }

far left The "Canada goose"—a signature lift for Virtue and Moir—displays their grace, strength, and balance. Virtue is poised on Moir's leg as he skates in a spread eagle.

left Virtue and Moir's creative lift at the end of their Free Dance was one of many highlights in their performance that reinforced their connection.

below Skating to Mahler's Symphony no. 5, Virtue and Moir perform a lovely transitional movement designed to set the mood. Their performance was seamless with masterful execution.

below Americans Meryl Davis and Charlie White received Level 4 difficulty and plus-3 GOE scores for this amazing lift. Davis rolled up and over White's shoulder to balance on his free leg while he skated on one foot.

right Skating to a Bollywood theme for their Olympic Original Dance, Davis and White showcase a transitional movement. Their program was wonderfully authentic in its interpretation of the theme.

far left Davis and White perform a creative transitional movement. At the Olympics and Worlds, this Free Dance demonstrated speed, risk, and unison, along with tender moments when the music called for it.

left Davis and White seem pleased with their Original Dance performance. Their twizzles were fast, close, and in unison, and their circular step sequence was the only one in the event to earn Level 4 difficulty.

below In their Bollywood-themed Original Dance at the Olympics, Davis and White perform a transitional movement exhibiting strong choreography and effective interpretation.

far left Oksana Domnina and Maxim Shabalin of Russia perform a one-arm rotational lift in their Free Dance—contentious because Shabalin used Domnina's belt as a support. The ISU has since implemented a deduction if part of a costume is used in this way.

above Costumed in skin tone with greenery and loin cloths, Domnina and Shabalin chose a controversial Australian Aborigine theme for their Original Dance. Their strong skating skills were not evident in this dance.

left Domnina and Shabalin's straight line lift shows two difficult features: Shabalin in a spread eagle and Domnina cantilevered with support on one leg. World champions in 2009, they won bronze at the 2010 Olympics.

right In their lively Moldavian folk dance, Tanith Belbin and Benjamin Agosto of the United States featured speed, energy, and movements in character to the music. Here they begin their circular step sequence.

below In their Olympic Free Dance, Belbin and Agosto perform a lift with two difficult features: Agosto in a low crouch with one leg to the side; Belbin in a ring position with her upper body arched and her free leg pulled close to her head.

far right Belbin and Agosto perform a creative lift at the end of their Free Dance. This lovely lift enhanced the theme of the program and was a highlight in its choreography.

far left Federica Faiella and Massimo Scali's Italian folk dance played to their home crowd at Turin, Italy. This curve lift has Scali in an inside spread eagle and Faiella in a layback position with no support above the thigh.

left Faiella and Scali's emotional Free dance at the Olympics was performed to "The Immigrants."

below At the end of their Free Dance, Faiella and Scali thrilled the audience with this creative element—she lifted him as he had lifted her earlier, but with a different entry.

below Faiella and Scali's Olympic Free Dance included this straight line lift with Scali in a full crouch and most of Faiella's weight extended in a horizontal line, both difficult features.

right Americans Emily Samuelson and Evan Bates perform a curve lift with two difficult features—Evan in a deep crouch with one leg extended to the side, and Emily in a Biellman position.

below In their Olympic Free Dance, Cathy Reed and Chris Reed of Japan show their line and extension as they begin a step sequence. Their music was from *Angels and Demons*—Chris played the angel and Cathy the demon.

right Nathalie Péchalat and Fabian Bourzat of France skated their Olympic Free Dance to "Kika" and music from *Requiem for a Dream*. It was a passionate and energetic program.

far left For their Olympic Original Dance, Sinead Kerr and John Kerr of Great Britain skated an American country dance to "I've Been Everywhere." Here, Sinead lifts John in a playful move designed to enhance the choreography.

left At the Worlds, Kerr and Kerr's Scottish Original Dance included this curve lift with John in a spread eagle and Sinead in an upside-down position with a challenging hold, both difficult features.

below Kerr and Kerr perform a lovely transitional movement as a link between elements during their Original Dance in Turin. It was beautifully phrased to the music.

right Isabelle Delobel and Olivier Schoenfelder of France skated to Jacques Brel's "La Quête." This straight line lift shows Schoenfelder in a spread eagle and Delobel leaning out with support only on her legs.

below Delobel and Schoenfelder perform a crowd-pleasing interlocked transitional movement. In this playful Free Dance, they both tried to earn the limelight—Scoenfelder trying to be a star and Delobel skating for her country.

far right In their Original Dance performed to French folk music, Schoenfelder jumps over Delobel in a fun transitional movement.

left Vanessa Crone and Paul Poirier of Canada perform a transitional movement at the beginning of their Worlds Free Dance. They skated a lovely interpretation of "Nocturne" and "Bohemian Rhapsody."

below Crone and Poirier practice a stationary lift. Poirier rotates in a deep crouch and Crone is in a ring with her free foot close to her head. The lift floated beautifully to the musical phrasing.

Triumph on Ice   127

below In their Worlds Free Dance, Anna Cappellini and Luca Lanotte of Italy perform a straight line lift. Lanotte skates on one foot in a deep crouch; Cappellini extends her body weight in a horizontal line.

right Alexandra Zaretsky and Roman Zaretsky of Israel skated their Free Dance to "Schindler's List." Here they are in the middle of a rotational transition movement that matched the music and helped to set the mood.

. . . . .

CONCLUSION: WHERE WILL FIGURE SKATING GO FROM HERE?

. . . . .

ONE POSITIVE result of the current judging system is that the focus is back on the skaters. Under the 6.0 system, there was too much emphasis on the judges and how they were scoring—sometimes the judges generated more news than the skating itself. Yet the skating and the skaters are what matter. It comes down to recognizing that the adjudicating must be fair and as concrete and objective as possible within a judged sport. The current ISU judging system facilitates that and allows our attention to return to the ice—where it should have been in the first place.

Where will figure skating go from here? It's anyone's guess. How much more can the human body do? Certainly the skaters who have grown up with the current system are more readily able to adapt to its increased physical demands. It is clear that while jumps are still important in Singles and Pairs, they are not sole determining factors of success. Ice Dance will change, as the ISU has made a decision to drop the Compulsory Dance and to reduce the event to two parts— Short Dance and Free Dance. Point values for elements will be adjusted by the ISU as the sport demands it. That will continue to drive training attention and focus.

It appears from the Vancouver Olympics and the 2010 ISU World Championships that Pair skating will remain strong in China. North American ice dancers

above Virtue and Moir execute a
spin during their Olympic Free Dance.
Moir is in a full sit position with Virtue
performing a layback while spinning.
This spin reflects their sensitive
program and the connection between
these long-time partners.

are more impressive than ever and are setting the trends. Russia is no longer the dominant force it was, and many Russian coaches have migrated to teach in the United States, leaving a void back home. Japan and Korea have strong emerging single skaters—look for more to come from those countries.

Figure skating has grown to embrace and reward all contributing facets of the sport and has been enriched by doing so. It has changed enormously with the impact of the current judging system. One wonders if future changes will be as dramatic or as dynamic as those of the past few years. The one thing we can count on is that figure skaters in all disciplines from around the world will continue to enthrall fans with their athletic feats and spectacular performances.

INDEX OF SKATERS
AND COACHES

Bold page numbers indicate photo or figure.

Abbott, Jeremy **94**

Agosto, Benjamin **27, 114, 115**

Amodio, Florent **102**

Ando, Miki 19, **75**

Anissina, Marina 1

Asada, Mao 20, 22, **64, 65, 66, 67**

Bates, Evan **31, 119**

Belbin, Tanith **27, 114, 115**

Bourne, Shae-Lynn 6

Bourzat, Fabian **121**

Březina, Michal **95**

Browning, Kurt 31

Buttle, Jeffrey 30

Cappellini, Anna **128**

Chan, Patrick **28**, 34, **88, 89, 130**

Cohen, Sasha 21

Crone, Vanessa 26, **28, 126, 127**

Davis, Meryl 1, 2, 22, 24, **25, 32, 33, 108, 109, 110, 111**

Davison, Bryce **56, 57**

Dean, Christopher 1, 22

Delobel, Isabelle **124, 125**

Domnina, Oksana **23, 112, 113**

Dubé, Jessica **56, 57**

Evora, Amanda **16**

Faiella, Federica 34, **34, 116, 117, 118**

Flatt, Rachael 22, **73**

Hay, Cody **17, 55**

Joubert, Brian 30, 34, 35, **92, 93**

Kavaguti, Yuko 14, 32, **52, 53**

Kerr, John **122, 123**

Kerr, Sinead **122, 123**

Khokhlova, Jana 23

Kim, Yu-Na **2, 3**, 19, **60, 61, 62, 63**

Kostner, Carolina **78, 79**

Kozuka, Takahiko **101**

Kraatz, Victor 6

Kwan, Michelle **20, 21**

Ladwig, Mark **16**

Lambiel, Stéphane 20, 34, **90, 91**

Langlois, Annabelle **17**, **55**
Lanotte, Luca **128**
Lepistö, Laura 8, 9, **76**
Lysacek, Evan 3, 7, 22, **32**, 34, 35, **36**, **37**, 38, 80, 81, 82
Moir, Scott 1, 2, **4**, 22, 24, **31**, 33, **104**, **105**, **106**, **107**, **132**
Mukhortova, Maria **58**, **59**
Nagasu, Mirai 10, **11**, **70**, **71**, **72**
Novitski, Sergei **23**
Oda, Nobunari 34, **98**, **99**
Pang, Qing **15**, 17, **44**, **45**, **46**, 47
Péchalat, Nathalie **121**
Peizerat, Gwendal 1
Pelletier, David 6, 31
Phaneuf, Cynthia **77**
Plushenko, Evgeni 3, 22, 30, 34, 35, **36**, **37**, 38, **83**, **84**, **85**
Poirier, Paul **26**, **28**, **126**, **127**
Reed, Cathy **120**
Reed, Chris **120**
Rippon, Adam **29**
Rochette, Joannie 3, 22, **68**, **69**
Ruh, Lucinda 19
Salé, Jamie 6, 31
Samuelson, Emily **31**, **119**
Savchenko, Aliona 2, 17, **30**, **48**, **49**, **50**, **51**
Scali, Massimo 34, **34**, **116**, **117**, **118**

Schoenfelder, Olivier **124**, **125**
Sebestyén, Júlia 19
Shabalin, Maxim **23**, **112**, **113**
Shen, Xue **viii**, 2, 17, **40**, **41**, **42**, 43
Smirnov, Alexander **14**, 32, **52**, **53**
Shpilband, Igor 1
Suzuki, Akiko **74**
Szolkowy, Robin 2, 17, **30**, **48**, **49**, **50**, **51**
Takahashi, Daisuke **22**, 34, **86**, **87**
Tong, Jian **15**, 15, 17, **44**, **45**, **46**, 47
Torvill, Jayne 1, 22
Trankov, Maxim **58**, **59**
van der Perren, Kevin 18
Verner, Tomáš **103**
Virtue, Tessa 1, 2, **4**, 22, 24, **31**, 33, **104**, **105**, **106**, **107**, **132**
Voronov, Sergei **100**
Weir, Johnny 18, **96**, **97**
White, Charlie 1, 2, 22, 24, **25**, **32**, 33, **108**, **109**, **110**, **111**
Zaretsky, Alexandra **129**
Zaretsky, Roman **129**
Zhang, Dan **54**
Zhang, Hao **54**
Zhao, Hongbo **viii**, 2, 17, **40**, **41**, **42**, 43
Zoueva, Marina 1

ACKNOWLEDGMENTS

SINCERE THANKS to Gérard Châtaigneau for his enthusiasm and love of figure skating and for sharing and capturing the sport's emotions with his brilliant photography. Thanks to our editors and those involved at Greystone for their spirited efforts on our behalf. Thanks to Benjamin Okolski for Pair technical clarification; to Lauren Senft for Ice Dance technical clarification; and to David Islam for his thoughts and perspective.

The following International Skating Union material was useful in my research: the ISU website (www.isu.org); ISU Special Regulations and Technical Rules: Single and Pair Skating and Ice Dance 2008; ISU Communications 1494, 1557, 1567, 1583, 1610, 1611; ISU Project Team material for the Development of Components and the corresponding Educational DVDs. —*Jean Riley Senft*

MY THANKS to Jean Senft for her unwavering belief in the sport and in this book. My thanks to the good folks at Greystone for giving us this opportunity. My thanks to the people of Vancouver for being such great Olympic hosts, and to the many who, during the Games, were so gracious in helping to solve whatever problems arose.—*Gérard Châtaigneau*

RHODERICK MATIAS LISING

JEAN RILEY SENFT is an International Skating Union World and Olympic Judge and Referee and has worked with athletes for more than forty years. A member of the Canadian Olympic Committee and a Board Director of the Canadian Olympic Foundation, in 2009 Senft was the inaugural recipient of the Sports Officials Canada Integrity Award, which was thereafter named in her honour—the Jean Riley Senft Integrity Award. She has won several other awards, including the 2008 Women in Sport Award from the Minerva Foundation for BC Women. She lives in West Vancouver, Canada.

GÉRARD CHÂTAIGNEAU

GÉRARD CHÂTAIGNEAU is a photographer and former figure skater. He has been photographing skating for more than twenty years, including all the Olympics and World Championships since 1988. He lives in Toronto, Canada.